THE RESPIRATORY SYSTEM

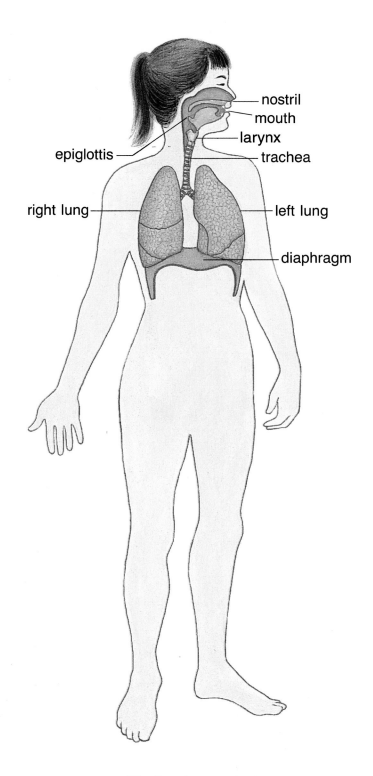

nostril

mouth

larynx

trachea

epiglottis

right lung

left lung

diaphragm

The Respiratory System

HUMAN BODY SYSTEMS

THE RESPIRATORY SYSTEM

DR. ALVIN, VIRGINIA, AND ROBERT SILVERSTEIN

TWENTY-FIRST CENTURY BOOKS

Brookfield, Connecticut

Twenty-First Century Books
A Division of The Millbrook Press
2 Old New Milford Road
Brookfield, CT 06804

Library of Congress Cataloging-in-Publication Data
Silverstein, Alvin.
Respiratory system / Alvin, Virginia, and Robert Silverstein. — 1st ed.
p.   cm. — (Human body systems)
Includes index.
1. Respiration—Juvenile literature. 2. Respiratory organs—Juvenile literature.
[1. Respiratory system. 2. Respiration.] I. Silverstein, Virginia B. II. Silverstein, Robert A.
III. Title. IV. Series.
QP121.S547 1994
612.2—dc20   94-21422
                                                                              CIP
                                                                              AC

Printed in Hong Kong
ISBN 0-8050-2831-5

10 9 8 7 6

Drawings by Lloyd Birmingham

Photo Credits

Cover: Howard Sochurek/The Stock Market

pp. 11, 77: National Aeronautics and Space Administration; p. 13: Tom McHugh/Photo Researchers, Inc.; p. 17 (l): Jean-Loup Charmet/Science Photo Library/Photo Researchers, Inc.; pp. 17 (r), 65 (r): Science Photo Library/Photo Researchers, Inc.; p. 26: Art Seitz/Liaison International; p. 27: Richard Hutchings/Photo Researchers, Inc.; p. 31: National Coal Association; p. 33: Joseph Nettis/Photo Researchers, Inc.; p. 39 (r): Ydav Levy/Phototake; p. 39 (b): Bud Lehnhausen/Photo Researchers, Inc.; pp. 46, 72, 73: Environmental Protection Agency; p. 49: Linda Steinmark/Custom Medical Stock Photo; p. 54: Dave Weintraub/Photo Researchers, Inc.; p. 55: Anthony Mercieca/Photo Researchers, Inc.; p. 57: Ronald H. Cohn/The Gorilla Foundation; p. 61 (l): Constance Porter/Photo Researchers, Inc.; p. 61 (r): Ralph C. Eagle/Photo Researchers, Inc.; p. 61 (b): Dr. J. Burgess/Science Photo Library/Photo Researchers, Inc.; p. 63 (l): Dr. Kari Lounatmaa/Science Photo Library/Photo Researchers, Inc.; p. 63 (r): Alfred Pasieka/Science Photo Library/Photo Researchers, Inc.; p. 65 (l): Biophoto Associates/Science Source/Photo Researchers, Inc.; p. 68: Jeff Isaac Greenberg/Photo Researchers, Inc.; p. 69: Hans Halberstadt/Photo Researchers, Inc.; p. 70: Simon Fraser/RVI, Newcastle-Upon-Tyne/Science Photo Library/Photo Researchers, Inc; p. 75: Andrew Martinez/Photo Researchers, Inc.

CONTENTS

SECTION 1

AIR FOR LIFE

If you hold your hand in front of your nose and mouth, you will feel puffs of warm air. This is the air that you have just breathed out of your lungs. After each of these puffs, you breathe in again and fill your lungs with new air.

You will probably take more than 700 million breaths of air in your lifetime—close to 30,000 breaths each day. A person does not have to think about breathing. We breathe in and out when we are asleep, just as we do when we are awake.

It is fortunate that breathing goes on so automatically—we could not live without it. Breathing brings in air, which contains a gas called **oxygen.** Our bodies, just like those of almost all living creatures, need oxygen to live and grow.

WHAT IS AIR?

You can't see air and (usually) you can't smell it. But you can feel it when it is moving in a breeze or wind. Air is a mixture of colorless gases: it is nearly four-fifths nitrogen and one-fifth oxygen, with small amounts of other gases such as carbon dioxide and water vapor. The air we breathe also contains tiny bits of dust, plant pollen grains, and other solid particles.

All the living things of the earth, from huge whales to tiny insects, from tall trees to the green scum floating on a pond, are made up of microscopic building blocks called cells. Each cell is like a busy chemical factory.

Thousands of different events are going on in each cell of every living thing all the time.

A factory burns fuel, such as oil or coal, to power its production. Living cells use food materials as the fuel to power their activities. They get energy from food materials by combining them with oxygen in a process called **respiration.**

For some plants and animals, getting oxygen to the body cells is very simple. But others, including humans, have complex **respiratory systems** to take in oxygen from air or water and deliver it to the body cells.

HOW BIG?

If you had to breathe through your skin, you would have a total surface area of only about 90 square feet (8 square meters) for gases to pass through. You might think that the lungs, which take up only part of the body, would have an even smaller surface area. But the gas exchange in the lungs takes place through the thin walls of the alveoli. These air sacs are tiny, but their total surface area adds up to about 1,000 square feet (90 square meters)—enough to cover a tennis court!

PART OF NATURE'S CYCLE

Our planet is surrounded by a layer of gases called the **atmosphere**. Most of the gases in the atmosphere are of no use to us. For example, the air we breathe out contains just as much nitrogen as the air we breathe in, because we cannot use nitrogen in our bodies. But we do use oxygen, to get energy from foods. In our body cells, this respiration process uses up oxygen and produces another gas, **carbon dioxide**, as a by-product. So the air we breathe out contains less oxygen and more carbon dioxide than the air we breathed in. Fires also use up oxygen and produce carbon dioxide—and in our modern world with car engines and the furnaces of homes and factories, there are a lot of fires burning.

And yet the mixture of gases in the atmosphere remains in just about the same proportions. Why doesn't all the oxygen in the atmosphere get used up? What happens to all the carbon dioxide we and other living things keep breathing out?

The gases in our air are kept in balance by the living things of our world. When we breathe, we take oxygen from the atmosphere and add carbon dioxide to it. But meanwhile, plants are doing something else to change the mixture of gases.

The green plants of our world need oxygen to live, just as we do, but they also take in large amounts of carbon dioxide. In sunlight they combine this gas with water to form sugars, starches, and other more complicated chemicals. This process is called **photosynthesis.** Oxygen is released into the air as a by-product of this process.

Plants can photosynthesize only during the day or under artificial lights. But they "breathe"—in the process known as respiration—all the time. Even so, the amount of carbon dioxide they use up in photosynthesis is much more than they produce. And they give off much more oxygen

*The gases that make up the earth's atmosphere are
kept in balance by the activities of plants and animals.*

than they take in. So plants help to replace the oxygen that the animals of the earth use up.

Plants and animals need each other to keep the cycle of gases in balance. Plants cannot make their food without the carbon dioxide that animals breathe out. (The plants' own respiration alone would not supply enough.) And animals could not breathe without the oxygen produced by photosynthesizing plants.

HOW PLANTS AND ANIMALS BREATHE

All living creatures, except for a few types of microorganisms, need oxygen to live. The simplest creatures absorb gases right through their outer surface. That is how microscopic one-celled organisms take in oxygen and get rid of carbon dioxide.

Plants have tiny openings called **stomata** on the undersides of leaves and on stems. These openings open and close to allow gases to flow in and out. Oxygen can also enter through the roots by dissolving in a film of moisture that surrounds tiny root hairs and then passing into the root.

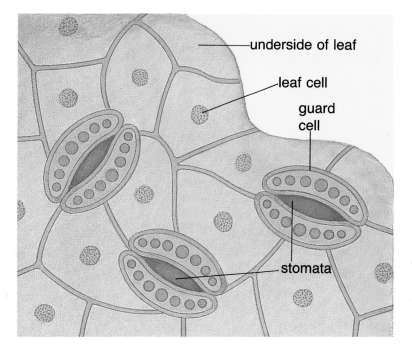

underside of leaf

leaf cell

guard cell

stomata

Tiny openings on the undersides of a plant's leaves are a part of the plant's respiratory system. The openings, called stomata, allow the plant to exchange gases with the surrounding air.

Insects also have a fairly simple system for respiration. Air passes through many holes called **spiracles** in the sides of an insect's body. The holes lead into air pipes called **tracheal tubes.** These tubes branch off to all parts of the insect's body.

CAN GRASSHOPPERS GROW TEN FEET TALL?

Insect monsters in the movies can grow to giant size. But in real life this could never happen. An insect is built something like Swiss cheese. Its respiratory system is made up of countless holes and channels running through its body. If an insect got too large, it would collapse, because there would be too much empty space inside and not enough structure to support it.

Earthworms breathe through their skins, too. But they cannot take oxygen directly out of the air. They must keep moist so that oxygen can dissolve in a thin film of water on their skin.

Larger animals need special organs to take in oxygen and deliver it to all their body cells. Fish, clams, octopuses, and other water animals have

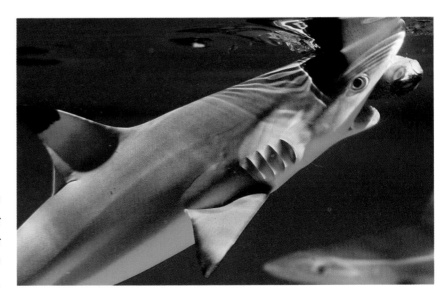

Sharks breathe underwater by means of gills, visible here as a series of slits in the sides of the shark.

special underwater breathing organs called **gills.** Water passes over thin membranes in the gills, which are lined with many tiny blood vessels. Oxygen molecules enter the blood vessels and are then carried through the animal's body to supply all its cells.

Frogs are unusual animals. They are amphibians, spending part of their life in the water and part on land. Frogs can breathe air through their skin. But they can't get enough oxygen in this way, so they also have special respiratory organs. When they first hatch into tadpoles, they swim in the

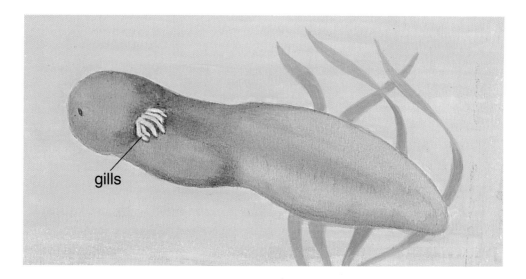

gills

*A tadpole breathes through gills until it
becomes a frog, when it develops lungs.*

water and breathe with gills. But when they turn into frogs, they grow new respiratory organs called **lungs** that allow them to breathe on land.

Most land animals, from snakes and lizards to cats and birds, have lungs. So do humans. Whales and dolphins have lungs, too, even though they live in the water. If they cannot come up to the surface to breathe, they will drown.

The inner surface of the lungs is kept moist. Oxygen gas from the atmosphere dissolves in the thin film of moisture and passes into blood vessels to be carried to all parts of the animal's body.

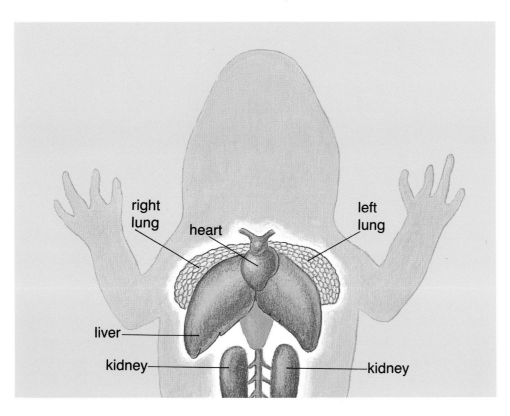

The respiratory system of a frog

ANIMAL RESPIRATION RATES	
Locust	1,020/min
Frog	120/min
Hamster	100/min
Hamster, hibernating	2/min
Cat	26/min
Woodchuck	25/min
Woodchuck, hibernating	12/hour

A sperm whale can go more than one hour without breathing. When it comes up to breathe, it inhales for two seconds.

CHANGING IDEAS

Since earliest times, people have thought of breathing as the most basic sign of life. Many ancient religions taught that the gods breathed life into people. The Old Testament says that "God formed man of dust from the ground, and breathed into his nostrils the breath of life."

Ancient people knew that living things need air to live, but they weren't sure what air was. Greek philosophers believed that air was one of the four basic elements that made up our world. (The others were earth, fire, and water.) Aristotle, a famous Greek philosopher who lived in the fourth century B.C., said that the heart was like a fire that heated the body with blood. We breathe in air, he claimed, to cool the heart down so that our bodies won't burn up. In the second century A.D., the Roman physician Galen firmly established the idea that *pneuma* (from the Greek word for "breath") was a spirit that came from the air and brought life to all living things.

People continued to believe that air was a spirit for nearly 1,500 years! It wasn't until 1643 that a young Italian scientist, Evangelista Torricelli, proved that air had weight and took up space.

Scientists began to make many more discoveries about how the body works and the way air gives us life. In seventeenth-century England, Robert Hooke found that parts of the body act as pumps, and John Mayow showed that the substance in air that animals need is the same substance that makes a fire burn. About a hundred years later, in 1771, the Swedish chemist Carl Scheele discovered oxygen. Soon after that, the French chemist Antoine Lavoisier figured out that oxygen was the component in air that we need to breathe. He believed that oxygen helped to burn substances inside the body, probably in the lungs or the blood. About a hundred years later a German scientist, Eduard Pflueger, showed that this

Antoine Laurent Lavoisier   *John Haldane*

"burning" actually occurs in body tissues. Meanwhile, the French researcher Claude Bernard figured out how oxygen is delivered to the body cells: it is carried in the red blood cells.

In England, John Haldane studied how breathing occurs and developed methods for determining how much oxygen and carbon dioxide are present in the blood and lungs. In the early twentieth century, the German scientist Otto Warburg studied how the body tissues use oxygen to get energy from food, and a British researcher, Joseph Barcroft, found out how oxygen passes from the lungs into the blood.

SECTION 2

OUR RESPIRATORY SYSTEM

The gateways to our respiratory system are the **nose** and mouth. The passages from the nose and mouth meet in a chamber called the **pharynx**. The pharynx leads into two new passageways. One is open, but the other is guarded by a trapdoor called the **epiglottis**. The open passageway, called the esophagus, leads down into the stomach. The guarded passageway, called the **trachea**, leads down to the lungs.

At the top of the trachea, just under the epiglottis, there is a widened chamber. This is the **voice box,** or **larynx,** which enables us to make sounds and speak. Going downward, the trachea branches into two small-

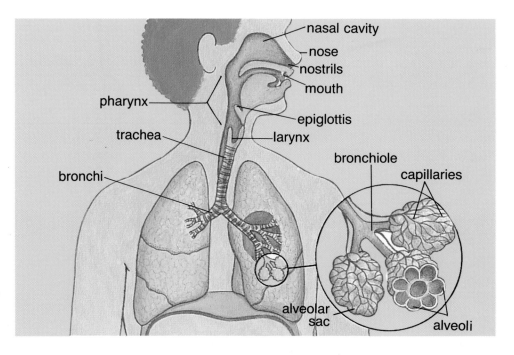

The air passages of the nose and mouth lead down into the pulmonary tree.

er passageways called bronchi. One leads into the left lung and the other into the right lung. Each **bronchus** branches again and again into smaller and smaller passageways, the tiniest of which are called **bronchioles.**

Each bronchiole ends in a little air-filled sac called an **alveolus.** These alveoli are grouped together in clusters like bunches of grapes. There are millions and millions of them, and together they make up our lungs. If we could take the walls of all the alveoli from a single pair of lungs and make clothing from them, we would have enough material to clothe over a hundred people!

The air we breathe in travels through the pharynx, trachea, bronchi, and bronchioles to reach the alveoli. Oxygen from the air passes through the thin walls of the alveoli into the bloodstream, where it is carried throughout the body. Meanwhile, carbon dioxide passes from the blood into the alveoli and is carried out of the body when we breathe out.

Both lungs fit snugly within the chest cavity. The lungs are protected by a cage of bones called the **ribs.** Below the lungs, a thick dome-shaped muscle called the **diaphragm** forms a floor for the rib cage and can move up and down. It plays a very important part in breathing. Other muscles, found between the ribs, also help us to breathe.

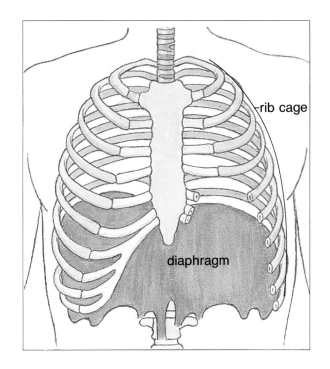

rib cage

diaphragm

AN UPSIDE-DOWN TREE

The airways, from the trachea to the lungs, look something like a tree. The trachea is the trunk, and the bronchi are branches that divide into smaller twigs (the bronchioles). That is why the airways are often called the **pulmonary tree.**

THE NOSE AND MOUTH

People's noses come in many shapes and sizes, but they all serve as an entranceway to the respiratory system. Air is breathed in and out through two openings called **nostrils**. If you look in the mirror, you can see bristly little hairs in the openings of your nostrils. These act as a sort of screen or trap: they catch bits of dust and other particles from the air and keep them from getting far into your nose.

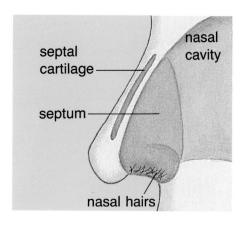

The nose has a lining called a mucous membrane, which helps to keep tiny particles out of the lungs.

Particles too small to be trapped by the screen of hairs in your nostrils are stopped farther along the nasal passages—they are caught in a sticky lining that covers the entire respiratory tract. This lining is called a **mucous membrane,** and the sticky substance it produces is **mucus.** When you have a cold, your body makes much more mucus than usual, and that is what makes your nose "run." The mucus also adds moisture to the air you breathe.

At the top of the nasal cavity, small patches of the mucous membrane contain special sensory cells that detect smells. They react to tiny chemical particles carried by the air.

Air enters through the nostrils into a large chamber called the nasal cavity. This cavity is divided in half by the **nasal septum,** a thin wall made of bone and a tough tissue called cartilage. Three flat, spongy plates called the **nasal conchae,** or **turbinates**, stick out into the cavity. They act like radiators and help to warm cold air. The bones that surround the nasal cavity

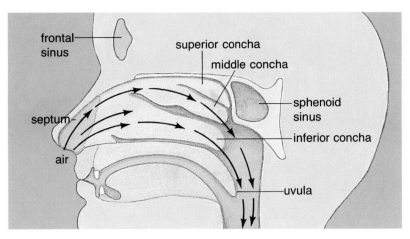

The main areas of the nasal cavity

contain hollow spaces called **sinuses.** They help to make the bones in your head lighter.

A flap of flesh called the **uvula**, at the back of the roof of the mouth, can seal off the nasal cavity and the airway down to the lungs. Have you ever had liquid back up into your nose when you laughed or sneezed while you were drinking? What happened was that the uvula didn't work quite fast enough to close off the nasal passages.

MOUTH BREATHING

Most of the time you breathe through your nose. You can also breathe through your mouth, but when you do you may notice a difference. The air reaching your throat feels much cooler and drier than when you breathe through your nose. The mouth does not have the nose's special equipment for moistening, warming, and cleaning the incoming air. Breathing through the mouth can help bring extra air into the body during exercising. And you may have to breathe through your mouth when your nose is stuffed up by a cold. Mouth breathing during sleep may result in snoring, as air forcing its way past the uvula makes a rumbling noise. You are more likely to snore when you sleep on your back because the uvula hangs down into the air passage in that position.

THE SENSE OF SMELL

The part of our nose that is involved with the sense of smell is actually quite small. Most of the nose is involved in filtering the air we breathe so it is safe when it reaches the lungs. The nose's smell area is the **olfactory membrane**, two small patches of yellowish gray tissue, each about the size of a postage stamp. They are found at the top of the nasal cavity, beneath the bridge of the nose.

The olfactory membrane contains tens of millions of **receptor** cells, sensory cells that are sensitive to chemicals that produce smells. (German

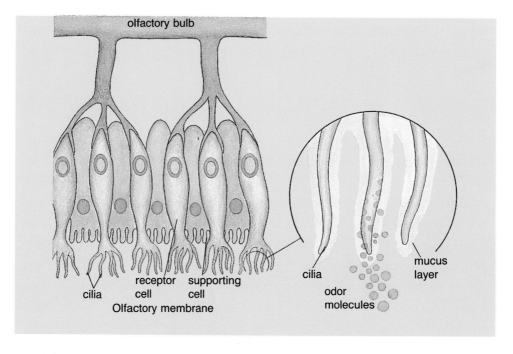

There are tens of millions of receptor cells in the olfactory membrane.

shepherds have about two billion smell receptor cells!) Olfactory receptor cells are actually nerve cells. Each one ends in a knob from which tiny olfactory hairs dangle in the gooey mucus. These hairs are like parts of an antenna reaching out for odor particles.

Mucus helps us smell. It protects the sensitive smelling apparatus in the olfactory membrane and also carries odor particles to the olfactory membrane. In order to be detected by the receptor cells, chemicals must be dissolved in a liquid.

Odor particles enter the nasal passage in the flow of inhaled air. They are absorbed into the gooey mucus and reach the olfactory hairs. The receptor cells are stimulated, and a message is transmitted to the brain. The brain interprets it as a specific smell.

How the brain knows exactly what it is smelling is still somewhat of a mystery. But people can recognize more than 10,000 different smells. Our sense of smell is also very important in helping us to taste things. When

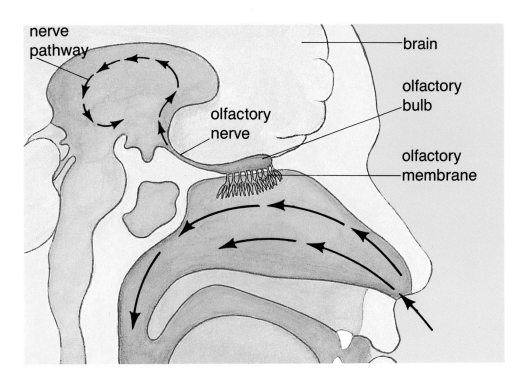

A smell is picked up by the olfactory membrane. It is then transmitted along the olfactory nerve to the brain.

Because of their keen sense of smell, dogs
can be trained to sniff out hidden drugs.

your nose is stuffed up by a cold and you can't smell very well, you find that foods don't have very much taste, either.

Scientists have discovered that the parts of the brain involved in forming memories are very closely linked with the parts that interpret smell messages. Memories of particular smells can last a lifetime, and a smell can often bring back a vivid memory. For example, the smell of cookies baking might make you remember a visit with your grandmother. Or the smell of blackboard chalk may make you think about school.

The senses of smell and taste are closely connected. Foods usually offer a wide variety of tastes and odors. But if your sense of smell is impaired, food will seem to have very little taste.

HOW WELL CAN YOU SMELL?

Have a friend blindfold you and then hold various items a few inches from your nose: for example, a piece of onion, a ripe banana, a flower, chocolate, cinnamon, cloves, a perfume bottle, pine needles, and a cloth moistened with a liquid cleaner containing ammonia. How many of the smells can you name?

THE AIRWAYS

Air breathed in through the nose or mouth passes through the throat or pharynx on its way to the lungs. At the back of the pharynx are two lumps of tissue called **tonsils**. They produce disease-fighting white blood cells and may become swollen and inflamed when you are sick.

From the pharynx air passes into the larynx, a chamber shaped like a triangular box, with walls made of tough cartilage. In some people the larynx forms a bulge that can clearly be seen in the front of the neck: the Adam's apple. Air passing through the larynx produces the sounds of the voice.

The trachea is a strong, flexible air tube, 4 to 5 inches (10 to 13 centimeters) long and up to an inch (2.5 centimeters) in diameter, that extends from the larynx down into the chest. Its walls are thick and muscular, strengthened by C-shaped rings of tough, rubbery cartilage. (You can feel the cartilage rings if you press gently with your fingers on the front of your neck.) The stiff cartilage rings keep the airway

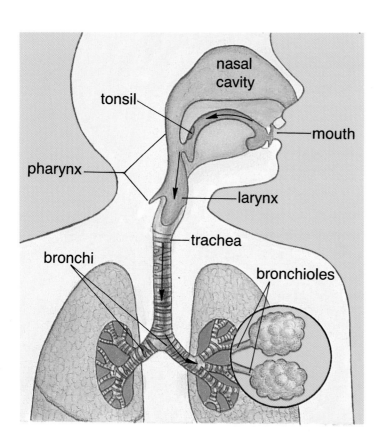

open, even when you turn your head or twist your neck. Muscles at the back of the tube can pull the open ends of the cartilage rings together to narrow the opening. These muscles tighten if something solid accidentally gets into the trachea, helping to keep it from slipping farther down.

Neatly fitted behind the trachea is another tube, the esophagus. It extends from the pharynx down to the stomach and acts as a food pipe.

The trachea divides into two narrower tubes called bronchi, which are also reinforced by cartilage rings. One bronchus passes into the right lung, and the other passes into the left lung. Inside the lungs, the bronchi branch again and again into smaller and smaller tubes. The smallest, the bronchioles, are only about 1/25 inch (1 millimeter) in diameter. Their thin walls have no cartilage support and are rather elastic; strands of muscles can contract to narrow their openings and cut down the flow of air.

SWALLOWING

The air you breathe, the food you eat, and the liquids you drink all pass through the pharynx, which has openings into both the air pipe (the trachea) and the food pipe (the esophagus). The epiglottis guards the opening into the larynx. Normally it closes during swallowing so that no solid or liquid will enter the airways. But sometimes, especially if you are eating too fast, the epiglottis may not close fast enough and a bit of food or liquid may "go down the wrong pipe." Then you cough and sputter until it is out again.

THE LUNGS

The two large, spongy lungs that take up most of the space inside the upper chest look like grayish pink balloons. The right lung is divided into three parts, called **lobes.** The left lung, which has to share its half of the chest cavity with the heart, is somewhat smaller and has only two lobes. Together, the two lungs weigh about 2 ½ pounds (1 kilogram).

Each lung is covered by two thin but tough and slippery membranes called the **pleurae.** One membrane is attached to the chest wall. The other surrounds the lung. These pleural membranes protect the lungs so that they can move a little while we breathe without being damaged by the ribs. The space between them is filled with fluid that makes them stick together. So when the chest muscles make the chest cavity expand, the pull on the pleurae makes the lungs expand, too.

Inside the lungs the bronchi branch up to 20 times, creating tiny bronchioles. At the tip of the smallest branches are bunches of thin-walled air sacs, or alveoli. Each lung contains 300 to 400 million alveoli. A network of tiny blood capillaries surrounds each alveolus. Gases pass freely through the thin membranes of the alveoli and the capillary walls.

The delicate walls of the alveoli are coated with a sort of nonstick chemical called a **surfactant.** This chemical keeps the walls from sticking together and makes it easier to inflate the air sacs, thus decreasing the effort needed for breathing.

Before birth a baby is suspended in liquid, and its lungs do not function. In fact, they are among the last organs to finish developing. The surfactant coating is not formed until the last month or two. This is why premature babies often have breathing problems. Doctors may treat such babies with an artificial surfactant or, if there is enough advance warning, the mother may be given hormone treatments to speed up the baby's lung development.

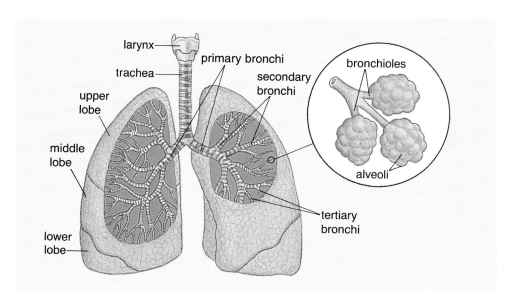

There are 300 to 400 million alveoli in each lung. These tiny air sacs exchange gases freely with surrounding capillaries.

In a newborn baby the lungs are a pale pink color. But they become darker as we grow older. Although the airways filter out much of the dirt and other particles, they cannot stop all of them. They cause the lungs to gradually become scarred. A miner's lungs may become hard and black after years of inhaling dust. Eskimos, however, live in a virtually dust-free environment, and their lungs stay pink for their whole lives.

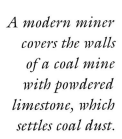

A modern miner covers the walls of a coal mine with powdered limestone, which settles coal dust.

THE CHEST

The ribs form a sort of cage around the chest cavity. These 12 pairs of flat bones are all hinged at the spine, and they curve around to the front of the chest. Most of the ribs are attached by flexible cartilage joints to a long, flat bone called the breastbone or **sternum**.

Except for the last two, each rib is connected to the ribs above with cartilage. All the ribs are attached to the spine, and most of them are attached to either the sternum or one another. So the cage is very sturdy. This also allows all the ribs to be raised at the same time.

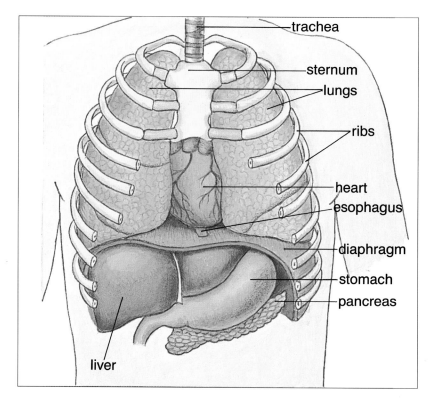

The ribs form a protective cage around the vital organs of the chest.

This huge dinosaur had a bony cage of ribs attached to its spine. As in a human, the cage protected its lungs and other vital organs.

There are muscles between the ribs. When more volume is needed in the rib cage—when we take a deep breath, for example—the muscles contract, or shorten. This pulls each rib closer to the next, which lifts up the entire rib cage. The volume, or amount of space, inside the rib cage is increased, allowing the lungs to inflate. Then when the muscles relax again, the rib cage returns to its normal shape.

The diaphragm is a strong dome-shaped muscle that makes up the floor of the chest cavity. It curves upward into the chest cavity following the curved line of the rib cage, just below the lungs. The diaphragm separates the heart and lungs from the organs in the abdomen. The stomach and liver are just beneath the diaphragm. Large blood vessels and the esophagus pass through it.

TRACING YOUR RIB CAGE

If you are very thin, you may be able to see the outlines of your ribs when you look at your chest or sides in a mirror. If you press gently on your skin, you can trace the outline of the sternum and the ridges of the ribs.

Place a finger firmly against one of your ribs and breathe deeply, in and out. Can you feel and see the movement of the rib cage?

SECTION 3

How We Breathe

The Air We Breathe

What Makes Us Breathe

The Gas Exchange

Where the Gases Go

Respiration in the Body Cells

Guarding the Respiratory System

HOW WE BREATHE

We have seen how air travels through the mouth or nose to the lungs, but how is air brought into the body?

The tiny particles, or molecules, of gases that make up air are moving constantly. They bounce about like tiny Ping-Pong balls as they bump into one another and into walls, furniture, or our bodies. Whenever they bounce, they strike with a certain force. The more molecules that strike, the greater the force. This force is called **air pressure.**

Usually we don't notice the pressure of the air molecules around us. But if there is a change in pressure, we do notice it. When you blow air onto your hands, you are forcing billions of extra molecules against your hand, and you are aware of the air pressure.

Inside our lungs the air molecules exert a pressure, just as they do in the air around us. Our lungs are like balloons, containing tiny bouncing molecules. Air pressure has a lot to do with how we breathe.

When the diaphragm is relaxed, it curves upward. When we breathe in, or **inhale**, the diaphragm tightens and moves downward, becoming flat. At the same time, the muscles between the ribs also contract. They pull on the ribs and bring them up and outward. With the floor moving down and the walls moving outward, the whole chest cavity grows larger. The balloon-like lungs swell, too. But the air pressure inside the lungs drops, because now there are the same number of particles in a much bigger space.

The pressure of the air in the room outside the body has not changed. Now it is greater than the pressure inside the expanded lungs. So air comes rushing into our lungs, until the pressure in them is again equal to the pressure in the outside room.

When we breathe out, or **exhale,** the opposite occurs. The diaphragm relaxes until it is an upward-curving dome again. The rib muscles relax, and

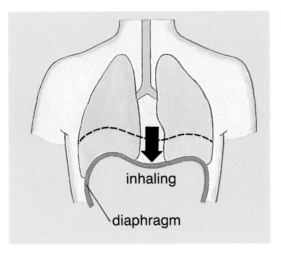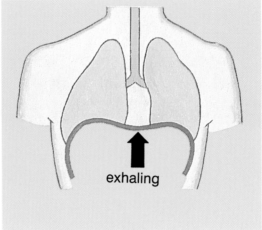

The diaphragm moves down and up during respiration.

the ribs move down. The chest cavity becomes smaller. The lungs are pressed inward, and there is not as much space for air molecules to move. The pressure inside the lungs rises. Now it is greater than the pressure in the room. Air is forced out until the pressures are equal again.

Inhaling is an active process that takes work by the breathing muscles. But exhaling occurs automatically and does not need muscle work. In quiet breathing the diaphragm does most of the work. But when you breathe deeply, your rib muscles are working hard.

HICCUPS

A hiccup occurs when the diaphragm suddenly contracts, causing air to rush into the lungs. The "hiccup" sound is produced when the **glottis**, the opening into the larynx, snaps shut. Excitement or eating too quickly can cause hiccups. You may be able to stop them by holding your breath or breathing into a paper bag.

THE AIR WE BREATHE

When you are breathing quietly, you inhale and exhale between 10 and 14 times a minute. With each breath, an adult takes in about enough air to fill a pint milk container. So an adult normally breathes in about 12 pints (6 liters) of air each minute.

During exercise, though, the muscles are working hard, and they need more energy—which means that they need more oxygen, too. So a person needs to breathe faster and deeper to take in enough oxygen to meet the active body's needs. In a deep breath an adult can inhale almost 4 quarts (about 3.5 liters) of air. During a hard run or a game like basketball, you may take in 15 to 20 times as much air as usual—more than 200 pints (100 liters) per minute for an adult. Even that may not be enough. The muscle cells use up the oxygen in the blood faster than it can be replaced, and you feel "out of breath." You begin to gasp and pant, taking short breaths each second or so. Even after you stop to rest, you will continue to pant for a while, until the muscles' temporary "oxygen debt" is paid off.

The lungs of an average adult man, breathing normally, contain about 6 pints (nearly 3 liters) of air—enough to fill up a big party balloon. But you can't blow up a balloon with one breath because close to 3 pints (at least 1.2 liters) of air stay in the lungs all the time. This amount is called the **residual volume.** Breathing very deeply can more than double the amount of air in the lungs. But no matter how hard you try, you can't blow out all the air in your lungs. And no matter how fast or deeply you breathe, not all of the "stale air" in your lungs will be replaced by fresh air.

Exhaled air contains water vapor, picked up from the moist lining of the lungs. When it is cold out you can "see your breath" because the water

In normal quiet breathing, inhaled air does not always reach all of the alveoli, and some may even close. A yawn is an unusually deep breath, through a wide-open mouth, which brings fresh air to all of the alveoli. People yawn when they are tired, sleepy, or bored—or when they see someone else yawning.

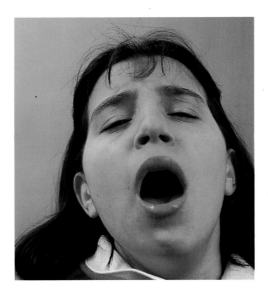

vapor condenses into a white fog. A whale's spout, which looks like a water fountain, is actually condensed water vapor, too. It becomes visible when the whale's warm exhaled breath hits the colder outside air.

Whales breathe through nostrils, called blowholes, at the top of the head.

WHAT MAKES US BREATHE

What makes the rib muscles and the diaphragm contract in the first place? A special part of the brain called the **breathing center** acts as a central signal station. It sends signals to the diaphragm and rib muscles to tell them when to contract.

How does the breathing center know when to send the signals? Carbon dioxide acts as a trigger. When there is a certain amount of it in the blood reaching the brain, it "tells" the breathing center that it is time to send out another signal.

You do not have to think about breathing; it goes on automatically. In fact, there are limits to how much you can consciously change how fast and deeply you breathe.

If you purposely breathe very rapidly and deeply, you soon begin to feel a little dizzy, and your breathing slows down. What happened? You were bringing a lot of oxygen-rich air into your lungs, and the amount of oxygen in your blood was increasing while the amount of carbon dioxide was falling. Soon the breathing center stopped sending out signals.

If you hold your breath, after less than a minute you will have a tremendous urge to breathe. Soon you will take a deep, gasping breath, no matter how hard you try to stop it. What happened? Since you were not exhaling, the amount of carbon dioxide in the air in your lungs kept increasing until it got harder for this gas to pass from the blood into the alveoli. Soon the amount of carbon dioxide in the blood was high enough to trigger the breathing center.

Breathing is also stimulated by conditions that increase the body's need for oxygen: exercise, breathing air with too little oxygen, a drop in the blood pressure, overheating, and fever.

The messages from the breathing center are sent along nerves to the diaphragm and rib muscles. The nerves controlling the contractions of the diaphragm run through a spot called the **solar plexus,** located on the front of the abdomen, just below the ribs. A sudden blow to this spot can stop the nerve messages for a moment. The person feels "winded" and is unable to breathe until the nerves recover.

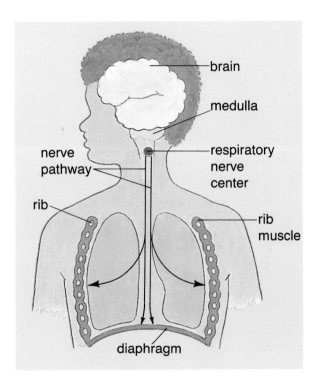

The breathing center in the brain controls respiration by responding to the amount of carbon dioxide building up in the blood.

BREATHING ACTIVITIES

How fast do you breathe? Count the number of breaths you take in a minute while you are sitting quietly. Then stand up and run in place for two minutes. Count the number of breaths per minute while you are running, and then count them right after you stop.

How long can you hold your breath? Try it, and write down how many seconds went by before you *had* to breathe. Then take six very deep breaths and immediately try holding your breath again. Can you guess why you were able to go longer?

THE GAS EXCHANGE

What happens to the air that is breathed into the lungs? It is drawn down into the millions of tiny alveoli. These air sacs, you may remember, have very thin walls—so thin that small molecules can pass right through them. You might imagine an alveolus as a basket made of chicken wire, in which Ping-Pong balls are bouncing. Some balls bounce on the wires, but others go through the holes.

Oxygen in the inhaled air dissolves in the thin layer of moisture that covers the inner surface of the alveoli. Some of the oxygen molecules flow through the membrane. After leaving the air sac, the molecules come to the tiny blood capillaries that are wrapped around the alveoli. These capillaries are too small to see without a microscope—so narrow that no more than one red blood cell can pass through them at a time. They are wrapped very closely around the air sacs, with a gap of only 1/25,000 inch (1 micrometer) between them. The capillaries, too, have thin walls, with gaps large enough for oxygen molecules to pass through easily.

Molecules of any substance tend to move from places where their concentration is high to places where there are fewer molecules of that kind. In the inhaled air the oxygen concentration is about 20 percent. But the blood flowing through the capillary network has already traveled through the body, delivering oxygen to the body cells. So its oxygen concentration is very low, and oxygen moves readily into the capillary blood.

Blood is pumped through the blood vessels of the body by the heart. As the blood flows along, each red blood cell normally spends only about three-quarters of a second in a capillary in the network around an alveolus. During exercise, when the heart is pumping harder, the blood moves faster, and a red blood cell stays in a capillary for only a third of a second. But that brief time is enough for each blood cell to pick up a load of oxy-

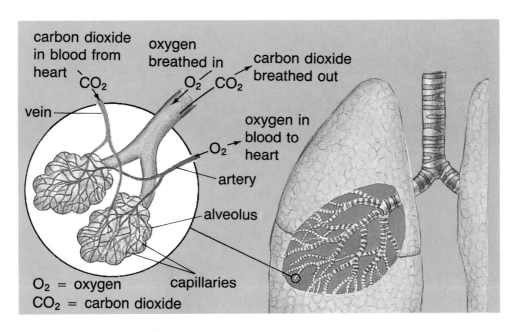

This diagram shows how oxygen and carbon dioxide are exchanged in the lungs.

gen, which combines chemically with a red substance called **hemoglobin.** (The combined form is called **oxyhemoglobin.**) About 280 million hemoglobin molecules are packed into each red blood cell.

The blood that flows through the lung capillaries is loaded with carbon dioxide, the waste product that was picked up from the body cells. Some of this gas is dissolved in the watery part of the blood, and some is combined rather loosely with hemoglobin. The carbon dioxide concentration in the blood is much greater than that inside the alveoli. So molecules of this gas flow out of the capillaries into the alveoli.

Thus, there is a sort of gas exchange inside the air sacs of the lungs. Oxygen in the inhaled air is exchanged for carbon dioxide, which is then exhaled. Meanwhile, carbon dioxide in the blood is exchanged for new supplies of oxygen.

WHERE THE GASES GO

The blood that flows out of the lung capillaries is bright red and rich in oxygen. (The bright red color comes from oxyhemoglobin.) This **oxygenated** blood is about to begin a long journey around the body. But first it must travel a short route, into the heart.

The heart is the pump that keeps blood moving through the body's blood vessels. It is divided into four compartments. The two upper ones, called **atria,** receive blood. The lower parts, called **ventricles,** are thick-walled muscular pumps, which contract to send blood spurting out through large blood vessels.

Blood from the lungs enters the left atrium and flows down into the left ventricle. This heavy-duty pump sends blood out through a very large blood vessel, the aorta, which divides and branches again and again into smaller and smaller blood vessels and finally into the microscopic capillaries. One or more capillaries pass close by just about every cell in the body, bringing food materials, oxygen, and various other chemicals.

As the blood in the capillaries flows past the body cells, another gas exchange takes place. It is exactly the opposite of the gas exchange in the lungs. Cells produce carbon dioxide as a by-product of their activities, so the concentration of this gas in the body cells is much greater than its concentration in the blood. Carbon dioxide passes out of the cells and in through the thin capillary walls to dissolve in the blood. The red blood cells are carrying oxygen that they picked up in the lungs. Oxygen and hemoglobin are held together rather loosely, and they readily come apart so that oxygen molecules can move into the body cells, where the concentration of this gas is much lower. Thus, carbon dioxide in the body cells is exchanged for oxygen from the blood.

The capillaries carrying blood from the body tissues merge into larger and larger blood vessels, which eventually empty into the heart. This

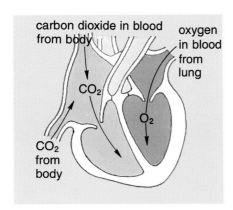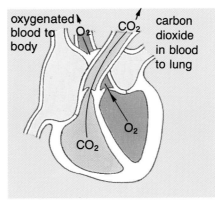

The heart is the body's pumping station. It sends blood with carbon dioxide to the lungs and oxygenated blood from the lungs throughout the body.

deoxygenated blood, with very little oxygen and a large amount of carbon dioxide, is a dull, dark, purplish color. It flows into the right atrium, then down into the right ventricle. At the next heartbeat, contractions of the ventricle wall send the blood to the lungs to drop off its carbon dioxide and pick up a new supply of oxygen. An average trip of a drop of blood from the heart through the blood vessels to the body tissues and back to the heart again takes less than a minute!

In the circulatory system, blood travels through two separate loops: oxygenated blood is carried from the heart around to the body tissues and back to the heart, while the same heartbeat sends deoxygenated blood from the heart to the lungs and back. The division of the heart into right and left compartments keeps these two flows separate, so that oxygen-rich and oxygen-poor blood do not mix.

DID YOU KNOW . . .

The cells in the cornea of the eye are the only body cells that do not have a blood supply. Blood flowing through the cornea would interfere with vision. Corneal cells get their oxygen directly from the air.

RESPIRATION IN THE BODY CELLS

Right now thousands of chemical reactions are going on inside the cells of your body. These reactions are helping you to sit up, move your eyes across the page, think about what you are reading, and do many other things. All these activities require energy, which the body gets from chemical energy stored in foods. But oxygen is needed to release food energy, in a process called **cellular respiration**.

In a way, cellular respiration is very much like burning. When you light a campfire, you need fuel to burn. But you also need air to keep it going. If you covered the fire with a glass dome so that no new air could get to it, the fire would quickly go out.

In a fire, fuel is combined with oxygen to release energy in the form of heat and light. The sticks and dry leaves burned in a campfire are converted to carbon dioxide or another product, carbon monoxide. But the fuel does not burn completely; part of it is left as black charcoal, which is carbon.

Cellular respiration uses fuel much more efficiently than a campfire. In a complicated series of steps, energy is released a little at a time and stored in chemical packets called ATP. No light is produced, and only a little energy is "wasted" as heat,

Exhaust contains carbon monoxide as well as particles. These contribute to air pollution and can be dangerous to our respiratory system.

which helps to keep the body warm. And no charcoal is left; all of the carbon is converted to carbon dioxide.

Carbon dioxide is a dangerous waste product for the cell. Too much can poison it. That is why the other part of the gas exchange is needed, and the blood carries carbon dioxide wastes back to the lungs to be exhaled. So it is not surprising that carbon dioxide, not oxygen, is the signal that stimulates the breathing center.

A DANGEROUS MISTAKE

Fires in furnaces, car engines, and other places where there is not enough oxygen available for complete burning produce some carbon monoxide. Like carbon dioxide, it is odorless and invisible. If a person breathes air containing carbon monoxide, it passes through the walls of the alveoli into the capillaries just like oxygen, and it, too, can combine with hemoglobin. But it is held very tightly. A hemoglobin molecule that has picked up carbon monoxide cannot let go. So it cannot pick up oxygen. If too many hemoglobin molecules are tied up by carbon monoxide, the blood cannot carry enough oxygen for the needs of the cells. So the person may suffocate, just as though there were not enough air to breathe.

The tissues of the brain and muscles are especially big energy consumers, so they need large supplies of food materials and oxygen. These tissues have a rich supply of capillaries to bring them the materials they need.

GUARDING THE RESPIRATORY SYSTEM

The air you breathe is actually rather dirty, even though the dust particles, germs, and other bits of matter may be too small to see. We have already talked about some of the defenses that help to keep the respiratory system clean and healthy: the bristly hairs in the nostrils that trap large particles and the sticky mucus that picks up smaller ones.

The cells of the mucous membrane lining the trachea, bronchi, and bronchioles have tiny hairlike structures called **cilia** on their surface. Under a microscope the mucous membrane looks like a wheat field. The cilia wave back and forth in rhythm. Their movement creates currents in the mucus, which are always directed upward, away from the lungs and toward the nose. Particles trapped in the mucus are swept along in the currents, up through the trachea, and into the throat. A particle that has penetrated one foot into the airways will be carried out within 15 minutes. Then the

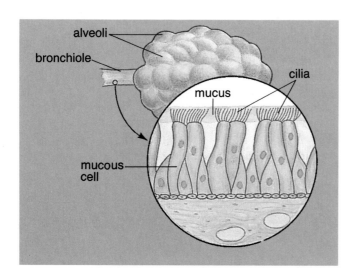

Cilia on the mucous membranes lining the airways produce currents in the mucus that sweep out inhaled particles.

mucus is swallowed and plunged into the acid contents of the stomach, where any germs are killed and pass harmlessly out of the body.

What happens in a **sneeze**? When the nasal passages are tickled by an irritant, such as a dust particle, nerve messages are triggered to make us breathe in suddenly, then breathe out explosively. During a sneeze, air travels at speeds up to 100 miles an hour. Mucus, solid particles, and anything else in the air passages are forcefully blown out.

In a **cough**, an irritant in the airways sends a message to a special cough center in the brain. This center makes us take a deep breath, of about 2 quarts of air. The glottis closes, and the effort to breathe out raises the air pressure in

Sneezing and coughing help clear respiratory passages.

the chest. The glottis pops open, and a blast of air explodes out of the mouth at a speed of 500 miles an hour, blowing particles and mucus out of the trachea and bronchi. In a heavy smoker or someone with a cold, the respiratory passages may become so irritated that the person coughs all the time. Some cough medicines work by soothing the air passages; others, such as codeine, act directly on the cough center.

Large white blood cells called **macrophages** wander through the tissues and literally eat up dust particles and germs. Their action is especially important in protecting the alveoli, which do not have cilia.

SECTION 4

THE VOICE

The main job of the respiratory system is to bring oxygen into the body and get rid of carbon dioxide. But the body can use the moving air streams in other ways as well. Breathing helps to bring us information about the world through chemicals perceived as smells. We can also use our breathing equipment to communicate with others by making sounds.

Air flows into and out of the respiratory system through the larynx, the hollow box of cartilage that sits at the top of the trachea. It is also called the voice box. Stretched across the inside of the larynx are two fleshy folds of tissue, the **vocal cords,** with a triangular opening between them. Air flowing through the opening makes the vocal cords vibrate when they are stretched tight.

During quiet breathing, the vocal cords are relaxed and do not vibrate

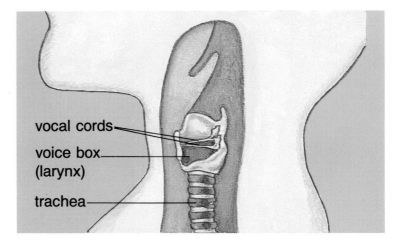

vocal cords

voice box
(larynx)

trachea

The main parts of the voice box

as the air flows freely through them. But when you want to make a sound, muscles of the larynx pull on the vocal cords, making them draw closer together. The tighter they are stretched, the higher the pitch of the sound. A singer continually varies the pitch of the voice, going up and down to follow the melody. Men typically have lower-pitched voices than women because they have a larger larynx with longer vocal cords. During adolescence, the voice box suddenly grows larger, especially in boys. An adolescent boy's voice may "break" sometimes, producing a squeak, because he is still learning to use his new, larger larynx. Irritation of the vocal cords can lower the pitch of the voice. That is why your voice sounds lower when you have a cold. Heavy smokers and drinkers may also develop a low-pitched voice.

Muscles in the larynx also vary the loudness of sounds by adjusting the size of the puffs of air coming from the vocal cords. Your throat may feel sore after you have been shouting because your laryngeal muscles are tired and strained.

We can make sounds either while inhaling or while exhaling. But usually we speak and sing only while exhaling and use the brief pauses between words or phrases to draw in a quick breath.

SOUNDS OF EMOTIONS

You sigh by drawing in a long, deep breath, then exhaling more quickly but forcefully. Usually the vocal muscles contract to make a sound while you exhale.

Sometimes it is hard to tell whether a person is **laughing** or crying. The respiratory movements are almost the same: the person breathes in, then breathes out in a series of quick, short puffs while the glottis is open and the vocal cords vibrate. Usually these two kinds of sounds express quite different emotions. But sometimes people cry when they are happy, and sometimes tears flow when they are laughing hard.

Sometimes you hear about a person losing his or her voice. In the 1992 presidential campaign, for example, Bill Clinton struggled with bouts of hoarseness that developed and roughened his voice during his many speeches. Finally, a few days before the election, he was suddenly unable to make a sound, and his wife, Hillary, had to finish a speech for him.

A variety of things can irritate the delicate mucous membranes in the throat, resulting in hoarseness or loss of the voice. For example, acids and other irritating chemicals in smog and cigarette smoke can damage the voice. In Bill Clinton's case, chronic allergies caused an increased flow of mucus. His vocal cords became irritated, and their vibrations were distorted. To further complicate matters, he had to breathe through his mouth because he had a stuffy nose, so his throat lining dried up. (Ironically, the antihistamines that people take for allergies also tend to dry out mucous membranes.) When he tried to continue speaking with irritated vocal cords, he added to the problem by tiring the vocal muscles. And so, he lost his voice.

Singers, actors, and others who use their voices a lot may develop nodules (small rounded masses of tissue) or larger growths called polyps on

Smog appears here in Los Angeles as a low-lying haze.
It contains chemicals that can damage the voice.

their vocal cords. These growths are normally harmless but can contribute to hoarseness.

Doctors and voice coaches advise that the best way to get over a bad voice strain is to rest the voice—either by not talking at all or by talking very softly. (But don't whisper—that is just as stressful on the voice as shouting.) Breathing warm, moist air from a hot shower or humidifier and drinking a lot of fluids can help bring the voice back to normal.

BIRD SONGS

A bird's voice is produced in a structure in its chest called the **syrinx,** or "song box." A bird's vocal tract allows it to sing two different melodies at the same time! Birds usually sing the songs typical of their own species, but some can also imitate the songs of other birds or even words from human speech.

A bird's song may be a way of communicating.

HUMAN SPEECH

Place your fingers against the front of your throat in the region of the larynx (the Adam's apple) and say "ah." Your mouth is open, and air moves freely out of your respiratory system. You can feel the vibrations in the larynx that are producing the sound.

Speech would not be very useful if all you could say was "ah." Yet that is all the larynx can do by itself. The sounds of the voice are shaped and changed to form words by the actions of the jaw, tongue, lips, and teeth.

Vowel sounds are made with the mouth open. Changes in the shape of the opening determine which vowel is spoken. Try saying the vowels *a, e, i, o,* and *u* in front of a mirror to see the different shapes your lips make. Blocking the flow of air with lips, tongue, or teeth produces **consonant** sounds like *b* and *p, d* and *t,* or *g* and *k.* Consonants called **fricatives,** such as *s, z, v,* and *f,* are formed by partly blocking the flow and forcing the air out through a narrow opening. **Nasal sounds** (*m, n,* and *ng*) are produced by sending air through the nose, with the mouth closed.

Babies learn to speak by imitating the words that people say to them. A baby learns to make the sounds of whatever language it hears, even though some languages include sounds that are not found in others. The German

CAN APES TALK?

An ape's voice box is high up in its throat, permitting its windpipe to be blocked off while it is eating or drinking. It can therefore swallow food or water without any danger of choking, but the kinds of sounds it can make are very limited. Although apes can learn to speak only a few human words, some have learned to "talk" in sign language, using their hands.

A gorilla is the largest ape. Here, a scientist is teaching sign language to young gorillas.

ch sound and the Scottish rolled *rr*, for example, are difficult to learn for adults who were raised to speak English. In a Bible story, Gileadite soldiers, defending a ford across the Jordan River, tested enemy suspects by having them say the Hebrew word, *shibboleth*. Ephraimites (members of the enemy tribe) could not pronounce the *sh* sound, so they said "*s*ibboleth."

In addition to the sounds produced by air flowing through the larynx, the flow of air through the nose and in the sinuses also contributes to the tones of the voice. That is why your voice sounds funny when you have a cold and your nose and sinuses are swollen and blocked.

In some languages, such as Chinese, the pitch of words is very important and can even change their meaning. Pitch is not as important in spoken English, but varying the tones when you speak helps to make what you say sound livelier and more interesting. Someone who speaks in a **monotone** (all on one level) usually sounds rather boring.

DID YOU KNOW . . .

The sound of your voice travels up the **eustachian tubes**, two narrow passages that connect the pharynx to the ears. That is the main reason your voice sounds so different when you hear a tape recording of it—you are listening only to the sounds that came out of your mouth.

BREATHING EMERGENCIES

"Don't eat too fast." "Don't talk while you're eating." This may sound like nagging, but it is good advice. Each year thousands of people choke to death. If something solid, such as a large chunk of food that was swallowed too quickly, gets into the trachea, it can block the flow of air into the lungs. Then there will not be enough oxygen in the blood to supply the body cells' needs. Brain cells are in special danger. If their oxygen supply is cut off for just four minutes, delicate brain cells start to die.

What should you do if someone who is eating suddenly gasps, starts to turn blue, and cannot speak? One good idea is to call for help. But there may not be time to find a telephone or wait for an ambulance. In 1973 Dr. Henry Heimlich suggested a simple first-aid method for choking that has saved many lives. The **Heimlich maneuver** forces the diaphragm upward, increasing the pressure inside the chest, so that whatever was blocking the airways pops out like a cork from a bottle.

Drowning, inhaling smoke, an electric shock, a heart attack, or brain injury can also cause breathing emergencies. People who have stopped breathing on their own can often be saved by various forms of **artificial**

THE HUG THAT SAVES LIVES

Stand behind the person who is choking and place your fist against the person's abdomen, just below the ribs. Hold your fist with the other hand and hug the person hard, pressing in and upward. If this Heimlich maneuver does not work the first time, try again until the obstruction pops out and the person can breathe. Striking the person sharply on the back between the shoulder blades may also help to clear the airway.

respiration, which deliver air to their lungs until they are able to start breathing on their own again. **Mouth-to-mouth resuscitation** is often called the "kiss of life." The rescuer tilts the victim's head back, pinches his or her nose shut, and breathes out to force air into the victim's mouth in a normal breathing rate (12 times a minute for an adult or 20 for a child). The extra carbon dioxide in the rescuer's breath may help to stimulate the victim's breathing center, and there is enough oxygen to supply the body cells' needs. If the victim's heart has stopped beating, too, a rescue team may combine pressure on the chest with mouth-to-mouth resuscitation, a first-aid technique called **CPR (cardiopulmonary resuscitation)**. But remember: *First-aid measures like these should be done only by people who have learned the correct techniques.*

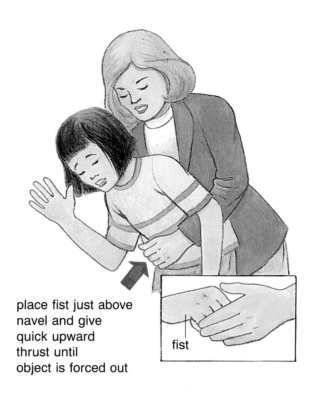

place fist just above navel and give quick upward thrust until object is forced out

fist

The Heimlich maneuver is used when someone is choking.

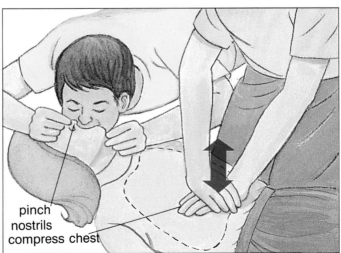

pinch nostrils
compress chest

How CPR is performed on an unconscious adult

BREATHING PROBLEMS

Do you sneeze every August or wheeze when you pet a cat? If so, you may be suffering from an **allergy** affecting your respiratory system. Allergies are actually mistaken efforts of the body to protect itself.

When germs or parasites get into the body, it can fight them in various ways. **Inflammation** is one of them: the cells that are under attack produce chemicals that cause fluid to leak out into the tissues, which swell and turn red. Macrophages, the roaming white blood cells that defend the body, can move about more easily through inflamed tissues, to catch and eat the invaders. Special chemical weapons called **antibodies** are produced, too. These defenses can help to keep the body healthy. But in allergies, the body mistakes dust particles, pollen grains, or other harmless substances for dangerous invaders. Things that provoke an allergic reaction are referred to as **allergens.** The symptoms that result from contact with an allergen vary depending on the part of the body where the mistaken defenses are put into effect.

Rhinitis is an inflammation of the nasal passages, which results in a stuffed-up, runny nose; sneezing; and watery eyes. **Hay fever** is allergic rhinitis that is caused by a reaction to plant pollens. Usually people with hay fever are allergic to the pollen of ragweed, grasses, or other plants—not hay. The symptoms occur at about the same time each year, when the plants are producing their pollen. The same kind of symptoms can also be caused by allergies to dust, to dust mites (microscopic pests that live on dust particles), and to the tiny particles that enter the air from an animal's saliva and fur.

In some people with allergies, the sensitive cells are in the mucous membranes deeper in the respiratory tract. Then exposure to an allergen can result in **asthma.** The linings of the bronchioles become inflamed, and the muscles of the breathing tubes may go into a **spasm** (a long, strong

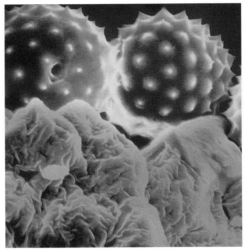

Ragweed   *A micrograph of ragweed pollen*

contraction). The airways become so narrow that it is hard to breathe. Inhalers that deliver drugs to relax the bronchial muscles can help to stop an asthma attack.

Cystic fibrosis is a hereditary disease in which the mucous membranes in the respiratory tract produce a thick, sticky mucus that clogs up the airways. Breathing is difficult, and frequent bacterial infections scar and weaken the lungs. In the past most children with CF died before adulthood, but now better treatments are helping them to

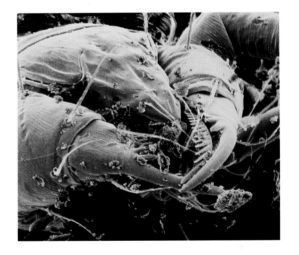

A dust mite, seen through a microscope

live longer. In 1989, scientists identified the gene involved in CF. The normal form of this gene can now be inserted into patients' lung cells. This is the first step in correcting the genetic defect that causes CF.

In **emphysema** many of the bronchioles are plugged up and the alveoli become enlarged and damaged. There are fewer working air sacs to provide for the vital gas exchange. People with emphysema feel as though they are not getting enough air and constantly strain to breathe. Smoking and air pollution can produce this breathing problem, which is becoming very common among older people.

RESPIRATORY DISEASES

Have you had a cold lately? According to health statistics, there is about a 5 percent chance that you have one right now. During your life, you can expect to suffer from between 50 and 100 colds!

There are a number of kinds of **cold** viruses, but they all attack the delicate mucous membrane lining the nose and throat. The miserable-feeling cold symptoms are not really due to effects of the virus; they are the results of the body's efforts to fight it. The stuffed-up, runny nose, for example, is caused by inflammation, aimed at helping white blood cells fight the germs more effectively. Fluid leaks into the tissues, and the mucous membranes swell, narrowing the breathing passages and producing watery mucus that helps to trap and remove germs. The nose feels sore when the swollen membranes press on nerves.

The runny nose is caused by the extra mucus, along with bits of damaged tissues and dead white blood cells. Coughing and sneezing help to clear this matter out of the airways. Inflammation in the sinuses may block their drainage and cause headaches. You can't smell very well because odor particles cannot get to the receptor cells in the swollen nasal membranes. A sore throat results when cells in the lining of the pharynx are damaged. Mucus-producing cells may be killed, causing the throat to become dry. If the virus attacks the larynx, you may have **laryngitis** and be unable to make voice sounds.

Colds may make you feel miserable, but most people recover within a week or so. **Influenza,** or flu, is a more dangerous respiratory disease. You catch it by breathing tiny virus-carrying droplets of moisture that people have coughed or sneezed into the air. The flu virus first attacks the lining of the nose and throat, but the infection may spread down into the lungs. The lung tissues damaged by the flu may more easily be infected by germs that cause **pneumonia.** In this disease, the inflammation and fluid fill the

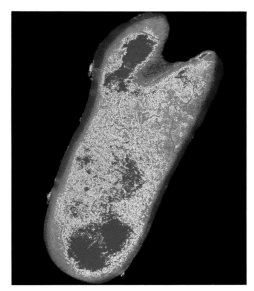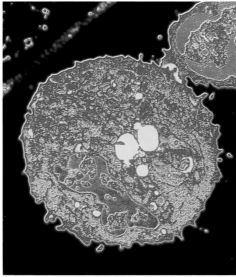

Tuberculosis and cancer both attack the respiratory system. Colored micrographs show a TB bacterium (left) and a human cancer cell (right).

alveoli and decrease the amount of oxygen that can be delivered to the body.

Sometimes body cells become changed and start to multiply wildly, spreading through the tissues and damaging the organs. This is **cancer**, and when it develops in the lungs it can be very deadly. Smoking and air pollution are major causes of lung cancer.

TB: AN OLD KILLER RETURNS

The **tuberculosis** bacterium infects lung tissue. At first the white blood cells may be able to keep the bacteria under control, and they are walled off in a hard, gray swelling called a tubercle. Later, TB bacteria may break free and start to infect lung cells again, producing symptoms like tiredness, weight loss, coughing, and spitting up blood. TB used to be one of the biggest killer diseases, but when effective drugs for it were developed it nearly disappeared. Now new, more dangerous TB bacteria are spreading, especially among people who live in crowded conditions and people with AIDS, whose body defenses do not work effectively.

EXAMINING THE LUNGS

Doctors have a number of ways to find out if there is a problem in the lungs. Perhaps you have wondered why the doctor places the end of a **stethoscope** against your chest and moves it around, asking you to breathe. The stethoscope is a rather simple device that gathers sounds and transmits them through a long, flexible tube to the doctor's ears. Healthy lungs make a soft, rustling sound as air passes through the airways. But when the lungs are infected, the doctor may hear crackles, whistles, or squeaks.

Have you ever seen someone tapping on a wall, trying to find a good place to hang a picture? You can tell by the sound which parts are hollow and which have solid studs behind them. A doctor may use a similar method of **percussion,** placing fingers of one hand against your skin and tapping them with fingers of the other hand. Healthy lungs sound hollow. In emphysema, when the air sacs are enlarged, the sounds are louder than usual. And when the lungs are partly filled with fluid, the doctor hears a dull sound.

LISTENING TO YOUR CHEST

With a stethoscope you can check out your own chest sounds or those of a friend. Place the sound–gathering end flat against the skin at various points on the front and back of the chest and listen to the breathing sounds. In some spots you will also hear the thumping sound of the heartbeat.

With a **bronchoscope** the doctor can actually look inside the lungs. This instrument is a thin, flexible tube containing special fibers that can transmit light. It is inserted through the nose or mouth and can light up the insides of the airways. The bronchoscope is also equipped with tiny tools so that the doctor can pluck out an object blocking a breathing tube, take a tiny sample of

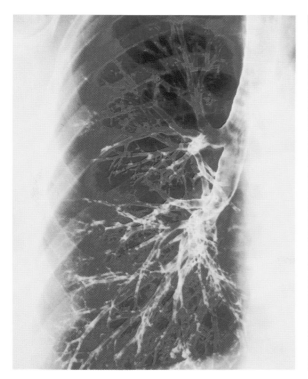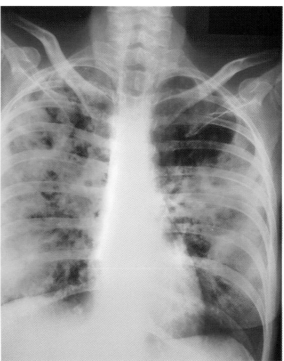

An X ray of a normal right lung appears at left. The X ray at right shows the results of tuberculosis (red areas) in both lungs.

tissue to test for infection or cancer, and deliver medications right to the spot where they are needed.

Chest X rays used to be a routine part of medical examinations. X rays pass more easily through some kinds of tissue than through others. So on an X-ray picture bones show up very clearly. The outlines of the heart and lungs can also be seen. Chest X rays also show up the hard tubercles that form in tuberculosis and various other kinds of lung damage. But too many X rays can harm body tissues, so doctors today use them only when they suspect a person has an infection.

When people complain of breathing problems, doctors may use a device called a **spirometer** to measure the volumes of air that move in and out of the lungs under various conditions. These tests are called **pulmonary function tests**.

SECTION 5

BREATHING AIDS

Sometimes people cannot get enough oxygen by just breathing air. People with emphysema, for example, may need to breathe through an **oxygen mask**, which delivers a gas mixture with a higher than usual concentration of oxygen from a gas cylinder. The higher oxygen pressure delivered by the mask helps this gas to pass more easily into the blood capillaries. In Tokyo, where the air is very polluted, traffic police take frequent whiffs of gas from an oxygen mask. A firefighter who has inhaled smoke inside a burning building may need to use an oxygen mask for a while. This kind of breathing aid can also help in treating people who have had a heart attack or are suffering from carbon monoxide poisoning or from shock due to loss of blood.

People who cannot breathe well enough on their own may be helped by a **ventilator,** a device that pumps warm, moist air into the lungs through a tube passing through the trachea. A computer monitors the amount and pressure of the gas pumped in and the amounts of oxygen and carbon dioxide in the air breathed out.

Before vaccines were developed to prevent **polio,** a disease that can paralyze the breathing muscles, patients were commonly treated with an older version of breathing machine called an **iron lung.** The patient's

A firefighter uses oxygen to help clear his lungs of smoke.

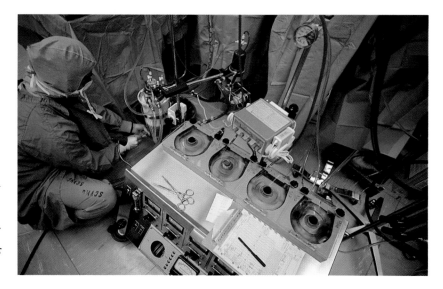

A heart-lung machine can take over for the heart and lungs during surgery.

entire body was enclosed inside a big metal cylinder containing a mechanical respirator that substituted for the work of the chest muscles.

Modern doctors can use an artificial lung if they need to operate on a patient's lungs or give them time to rest and heal. Blood is sent from a vein in the leg through a machine that adds oxygen and back through another tube into a large artery in the leg. A **heart-lung machine** includes a pump and can temporarily take over the work of both the heart and the lungs.

When lungs are too badly damaged to recover, surgeons may perform a **lung transplant.** Healthy lungs are taken from a person who has just died, perhaps in an accident, and are used to replace the damaged lungs of someone with cystic fibrosis or another serious lung disease. Special drugs must be given so that the person's body will not attack the foreign lung tissue. Sometimes a heart and lungs are transplanted at the same time.

TOO MUCH OF A GOOD THING

Sometimes pure oxygen is used in medical emergencies. But doctors have found breathing pure oxygen for too long a time can cause a buildup of fluid in the lungs, collapse of alveoli, and convulsions. At one time, pure oxygen was used to help premature babies breathe, until it was found that it can cause blindness. So lower oxygen concentrations are usually given for long-term treatment.

BREATHING DRUGS

The main job of the airways is to bring oxygen into the body. But this entrance into the body can also be used to deliver drugs, which may have good or bad effects.

Allergy and cold medications, which relieve congestion in the nasal passages, are often taken in the form of nasal sprays. A device called an **atomizer** squirts the medication right into the place where it will work, in the form of a fine mist. Medical scientists are developing forms of other drugs that can be delivered by nasal sprays—even insulin for diabetics. A problem, though, is that when nasal sprays are used too often or for too long a time, they may irritate and damage the delicate nasal lining. Asthma medications to relax the muscles of the bronchial tubes are usually inhaled through the mouth, using an inhaler called a **nebulizer.**

During a surgical operation, drugs called **anesthetics** may be used to make the patient unconscious, with no awareness of pain. Some anesthetics are injected into the bloodstream, while others are breathed into the airways. Ether, chloroform, and nitrous oxide (laughing gas) are anesthetics that are breathed in a gas form. Usually extra oxygen is added to the gas mixture because anesthetized patients may be so relaxed that they do not breathe very deeply.

A cystic fibrosis patient using a nebulizer to help loosen mucus in the lungs

Some people sniff airplane glue or inhale nitrite gases (poppers) in a dangerous attempt to get "high." Breathing chemicals like these can cause serious medical problems, brain damage, or even death.

Cocaine, an illegal drug that some people use to get high, is available in a powdered form that is snorted into the nose and absorbed through the mucous membrane or in a crystalline form (crack) that is smoked. At first, using cocaine may make a person feel wonderful. But after the drug wears off, there is a feeling of deep depression. The user may become addicted and continue to take the drug in order just to feel normal. In addition to its harmful effects on the body (some people have suffered fatal heart attacks), snorting cocaine also damages the nasal membranes, producing bleeding sores.

Marijuana is an illegal drug that is inhaled in the form of smoke produced by burning hemp leaves. Chemicals in the smoke pass into the bloodstream and travel to the brain, where they may produce feelings of pleasure but can also damage a user's judgment and thinking abilities.

The most commonly inhaled drug is legal (at least for adults) but can be very harmful. This is tobacco, smoked in cigarettes, cigars, or pipes or snorted in the form of snuff. The active ingredient in tobacco smoke is **nicotine,** a drug with powerful effects on the heart and blood vessels. But tobacco smoke also contains carbon monoxide (which, you may remember, can tie up hemoglobin molecules in the blood and keep them from carrying oxygen) and tars that can damage the delicate cells in the mucous membranes and lead to lung cancer. Tobacco smoke damages the cilia and the white blood cells that normally protect the airways, and it also prompts the production of extra mucus, which accumulates in the lungs and promotes the growth of harmful bacteria.

marijuana plant

HAZARDS AROUND US

Coal, oil, wood, and other fuels do not always burn cleanly. In an automobile engine, for example, the reactions of gasoline hydrocarbons with oxygen from the air may not go all the way to their end products, carbon dioxide and water. They also produce carbon monoxide, unburned hydrocarbons, and bits of pure carbon in the form of solid particles (**particulates**). Other chemicals in the gasoline form sulfur and nitrogen oxides, metal compounds, and various other products. All these chemicals are sent out into the air in the car's exhaust, adding to the air pollution. Sunlight may act on the chemicals in the air to form ozone and many other chemicals. All these ingredients can add up to a recipe for killer smog, like the fog in London that killed four thousand people in 1952. Communities are trying to clean up their air. Now there are laws requiring special converters on car engines to burn gasoline more completely and scrubbers to take particulates and other waste products out of the smoke from factory smokestacks.

A smog condition just outside Washington, D. C.

Everybody finds it harder to breathe on days when the air pollution is high, but young babies, the elderly, and people with asthma, emphysema, and other respiratory problems suffer most. Some become ill or even die.

People who work in certain jobs face special breathing hazards. Miners who breathe in tiny particles of coal dust or silica may develop black lung disease or **silicosis,** with coughing, chest pain, shortness of breath, and finally an early death. Other particulates that can harm workers' lungs include asbestos, cotton fibers, sugar cane dust, and fungus spores from moldy hay or mushrooms. Wearing a mask to filter out dust particles while working in dusty places can help protect the lungs.

You may not even be safe at home. Formaldehyde and other chemicals may leak out of building materials. Some rocks and soils contain uranium, which forms a radioactive gas, **radon,** that can seep into houses. In fact, many health experts believe that radon is one of the major causes of lung cancer.

Scrubbers on these smokestacks have removed many of the particles, so the smoke is mostly white instead of black.

SECONDHAND SMOKE

Smokers used to argue that they were only hurting themselves. But now it has been found that the tobacco smoke has harmful effects on everybody who has to breathe the air in a room where someone is smoking. Children living in a household where someone smokes, for example, have many more respiratory illnesses each year than children in a nonsmoking family. Many communities have passed laws forbidding smoking in public places such as restaurants, shopping malls, and government buildings. Some hospitals, schools, businesses, and transportation facilities also prohibit smoking.

BREATHING UNDERWATER

About two-thirds of our planet's surface is covered by water. We humans cannot breathe underwater because it does not contain enough dissolved oxygen. Scientists have made artificial gills from plastic membranes, but they are much too big and bulky to be practical. Generally, humans cannot stay underwater for more than a few minutes unless they take their own air supply with them.

Scuba divers breathe through a mask connected by tubes to gas tanks on their backs. The carbon dioxide they breathe out passes into the water and makes a stream of bubbles.

Deep-sea divers must wear special suits to protect them from the high pressures deep underwater. Below 200 feet (61 meters) they breathe a special gas mixture instead of ordinary air. Helium gas is substituted for part of the nitrogen in the air. A person breathing helium has a high, squeaky voice.

The nitrogen in the air we breathe does not seem to have any effect under ordinary conditions. But at high pressures, large amounts of nitrogen dissolve in the blood. Divers breathing ordinary air begin to feel happy and carefree when they get below about 120 feet (36.5 meters), but their judgment may be bad. Farther down they get sleepy, then weak and clumsy. They act almost as though they were drunk. This kind of nitrogen problem is called **rapture of the deep.**

SWIMMING UNDERWATER

You can hold your breath underwater for about a minute. If you take a number of deep breaths before going underwater, to fill your lungs with as much air as possible, you will be able to stay under longer.

Why doesn't water get into your nose through the nostril openings? When you hold your breath, your soft palate moves upward to close off the airway. Your nasal cavity is then filled with air, which prevents water from entering the airways unless you take a breath.

If a diver tries to come up from deep water too quickly, the nitrogen that was dissolved in the blood forms bubbles of gas. These bubbles may block blood vessels, cutting off the blood supply to tissues and causing a painful and sometimes fatal condition called the **bends.** So divers must be careful to come up slowly, or spend time in a decompression tank, which slowly lowers the pressure to the level at the sea surface.

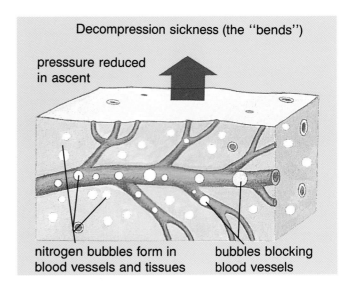

Decompression sickness (the "bends")

presssure reduced in ascent

nitrogen bubbles form in blood vessels and tissues

bubbles blocking blood vessels

Submarines, which travel underwater, are tightly sealed—not only to keep water out but also to keep in their air supply. Scientists think that some day people may live in huge, pressurized undersea domes, with a supply of trapped air so that no special breathing equipment is needed.

DID YOU KNOW . . .

Scuba stands for "self-contained underwater breathing apparatus." It was developed by Jacques Cousteau in 1943. Before then, divers had to get their air pumped through long hoses from the surface.

INTO NEW WORLDS

As you go up from the level of the earth's seas, either climbing a mountain or flying in an airplane, the atmosphere gets thinner. The higher you get, the less oxygen there is to breathe. Visitors to high-mountain areas, such as Johannesburg, South Africa, at 6,000 feet (1,800 meters) above sea level or even higher Bogota, Colombia, feel short of breath. Mountain climbers may have to take oxygen tanks with them. Yet natives of the Andes live up to 16,500 feet (5,000 meters) above sea level, and the Sherpa guides of Nepal do not need to breathe extra oxygen even when climbing to the peak of Mount Everest, nearly 29,000 feet (8,800 meters) above sea level.

People who live at high altitudes are adapted to breathing air with less oxygen. Their chests are enlarged, providing greater lung capacity, and their blood contains a higher-than-usual concentration of red blood cells, so they can carry a great deal of oxygen.

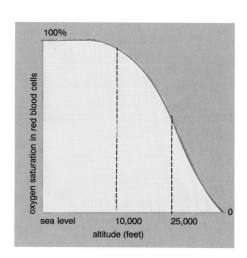

Airplanes can fly above even the highest mountains. Their cabins are pressurized to hold a higher concentration of air than in the atmosphere where they fly. Oxygen masks are available in case of emergency, if damage to the plane causes it to lose air pressure. These measures are not just a convenience; they are vital for safety. At 5,000 feet (1,520 meters), a pilot in an unpressurized aircraft becomes less able to make quick emergency decisions. At higher altitudes, pilots may lose consciousness. When the plane loses altitude, the pressure increases, and the pilot regains consciousness but is not aware of having blacked out.

Astronauts fly out beyond the earth's atmosphere, where there is no air at all. The spacecraft is pressurized and carries its own air supply. When astronauts spacewalk to do repairs on the outside of the spacecraft, they wear pressurized suits like those of deep-sea divers. An airlock, a small chamber with one tight-sealing door leading to the inside of the spacecraft and another opening to the outside, is used to keep the air inside the craft from escaping when an astronaut goes in or out.

Humans may someday travel to other planets that have an atmosphere with a different mixture of gases than ours. They may be able to adapt to the new conditions, if there is enough oxygen in the air. If not, they will have to carry an air supply with them.

An astronaut must wear a pressurized suit when working in space.

GLOSSARY

air pressure—the force exerted by gas molecules from the air striking a surface.

allergen—a substance that provokes an allergic reaction.

allergy—a mistaken reaction of the body's immune defenses against harmless substances.

alveolus—an air sac in the lungs. (Plural: alveoli.)

anesthetic—a drug that blocks pain sensations.

antibodies—proteins produced as defensive weapons against germs and other foreign substances.

artificial respiration—a first-aid technique for delivering air to the lungs when normal breathing has stopped.

asthma—a severe allergic reaction in which the linings of the bronchioles become inflamed and the muscles of the breathing tubes go into spasm.

atmosphere—the layer of gases surrounding our planet.

atomizer—a device that squirts out a liquid in a fine mist.

atria—the receiving chambers of the heart.

bends—disorder of deep-sea divers who come up too fast; due to blockage of blood supply to tissues by air bubbles in the blood vessels.

breathing center—the portion of the brain that controls breathing.

bronchioles—branches from the bronchi.

bronchoscope—a fiber-optic device used to look inside the lungs, take samples of tissue, and remove obstructions of the airways.

bronchus—one of the tubes branching off from the trachea and leading into a lung. (Plural: bronchi.)

cancer—a disease in which cells multiply uncontrollably.

carbon dioxide—a gas that is produced in respiration and burning and is present in small amounts in the atmosphere.

cellular respiration—the energy-releasing oxidation reactions that take place in living cells.

chest X ray—an X-ray picture of the chest, showing the outlines of the heart and lungs and various abnormalities such as tubercles.

cilia—microscopic hairlike structures on the surface of cells that wave back and forth, creating currents in the surrounding fluid.

cocaine—an illegal stimulant drug that is snorted into the nose.

cold—a viral disease in which the nose and throat membranes become inflamed.

consonant—a speech sound made with the lips, tongue, or teeth blocking the flow of air.

cough—an explosive exhalation through the mouth.

CPR (cardiopulmonary resuscitation)—a combination of pressure on the chest to pump the heart and mouth-to-mouth resuscitation.

cystic fibrosis—a hereditary disease in which the mucous membranes of the respiratory tract produce a thick, sticky mucus that clogs the airways.

deoxygenated—oxygen-depleted.

diaphragm—a dome-shaped sheet of muscle that forms the bottom of the chest cavity.

emphysema—an ailment in which the bronchioles are plugged, and the alveoli become enlarged and damaged.

epiglottis—a flap of tissue guarding the entrance to the trachea.

eustachian tubes—passages connecting the ears with the pharynx.

exhale—to breathe out.

fricatives—consonants produced with a partial blockage of airflow.

gills—breathing organs of water animals.

glottis—the opening into the larynx.

hay fever—seasonal allergic rhinitis involving a reaction to plant pollens.

heart-lung machine—a device in which blood from a vein is sent through a device that adds oxygen, removes wastes, and substitutes for the pumping action of the heart.

Heimlich maneuver—a first-aid remedy for choking that exerts pressure on the abdomen to force the diaphragm upward.

hemoglobin—the oxygen-carrying red pigment found in red blood cells.

inflammation—swelling of tissues due to leakage of fluid from damaged cells.

influenza—flu; a viral disease involving the nose, throat, and lungs.

inhale—to breathe in.

iron lung—a breathing machine including a mechanical respirator.

laryngitis—inflammation of the larynx resulting in inability to speak.

larynx—the voice box.

laugh—a sound produced by a series of quick puffs of breath through the larynx.

lobes—divisions of an organ, such as the lungs.

lung transplant—the surgical replacement of damaged lungs with the healthy lungs of someone who has just died.

lungs—the breathing organs.

macrophage—a white blood cell that eats up particles and germs.

marijuana—an illegal drug inhaled as smoke from burning hemp leaves.

monotone—speech of unvarying pitch.

mouth-to-mouth resuscitation—artificial respiration technique involving breathing into the victim's mouth while the nose is pinched shut.

mucous membrane—lining tissue that secretes sticky mucus.

mucus—a sticky substance that coats the inner lining of the respiratory tract and other body passages.

nasal conchae—turbinates; flat, spongy plates that stick out into the nasal cavity and help to warm cold air.

nasal septum—a thin wall of bone and cartilage that divides the nasal cavity.

nasal sounds—consonants produced by sending air through the nose, with the mouth blocked.

nebulizer—an inhaler that delivers drugs by inhalation through the mouth.

nicotine—the active ingredient in tobacco smoke, with powerful effects on the heart and blood vessels.

nose—entrance to the respiratory tract.

nostril—one of the openings into the nose.

olfactory membrane—portions of the nasal lining sensitive to odors.

oxygen—a gas in the atmosphere that supports oxidation reactions including burning and respiration.

oxygen mask—a device that delivers oxygen in a higher than normal concentration.

oxygenated—enriched with oxygen.

oxyhemoglobin—hemoglobin combined with oxygen.

particulates—solid particles of air pollution.

percussion—tapping; a technique used to detect abnormal lung sounds indicating the presence of fluid in the alveoli.

pharynx—the common passageway leading from the nose and mouth to the trachea and esophagus.

photosynthesis—the production of sugars and other complex chemicals by combining carbon dioxide and water in sunlight.

pleurae—the membranes covering the lungs.

pneumonia—infection of lung tissues by bacteria or viruses.

polio (poliomyelitis)—a viral disease that can result in paralysis of the breathing muscles.

pulmonary function tests—tests of breathing volumes used to assess lung health.

pulmonary tree—the airways of the respiratory tract.

radon—a radioactive gas that is released from rocks and soil and can damage the lungs.

rapture of the deep—impairment of brain function due to breathing nitrogen under pressure.

receptor—a sensory cell.

residual volume—the amount of air remaining in the lungs after exhalation.

respiration—the release of energy in living organisms by combining food materials with oxygen.

respiratory system—the organs involved in respiration, from nose to lungs.

rhinitis—inflammation of the nasal passages.

ribs—curving, flat bones that form the chest cavity.

scuba—self-contained underwater breathing apparatus.

secondhand smoke—tobacco combustion products breathed in by people around the smoker.

silicosis—black lung disease; lung damage due to inhaling coal dust or rock particles.

sinus—a hollow space; one of the hollow spaces in the bones surrounding the nasal cavity.

sneeze—a sudden, explosive exhalation through the nose.

solar plexus—an area on the front of the upper abdomen where the nerves controlling contractions of the diaphragm pass close to the surface.

spasm—a long, strong muscle contraction.

spiracle—a breathing opening in an insect's body.

spirometer—a device used to measure breathing volumes.

sternum—the breastbone.

stethoscope—a sound-magnifying device used to examine the heart and lungs.

stomata—openings on the underside of a plant leaf or on a stem (sing. stoma).

surfactant—a chemical that keeps wet surfaces from sticking together.

syrinx—the sound-producing "song box" in the throat of birds.

tonsils—lumps of tissue at the back of the pharynx that produce disease-fighting white blood cells.

trachea—"air pipe"; the muscular tube in the throat leading to the lungs.

tracheal tubes—air passages in an insect's body.

tuberculosis (TB)—a bacterial disease that damages the lungs.

turbinates—nasal conchae; flat, spongy plates that stick out into the nasal cavity and help to warm cold air.

uvula—a flap of flesh at the back of the roof of the mouth that can seal off the nasal cavity.

ventilator—a device that pumps warm, moist air into the lungs through a tube inserted into the trachea.

ventricles—the pumping chambers of the heart.

vocal cords—fleshy folds of tissue in the larynx that vibrate, producing sound when air passes through the opening between them.

voice box—the larynx; the sound-producing structure at the top of the trachea.

vowel—a speech sound made with the mouth open.

TIMELINE

B.C.

2700 Ancient Egyptians believed air carried a vital spirit into the body during breathing.

450 Empedocles (Greek) said air was one of the four basic elements that made up the world.

350 Aristotle (Greek) said we breathe air to cool down the fire in the heart.

326 Plutarch (Greek) described altitude sickness.

A.D.

160 Galen (Roman) said air (*pneuma*) mixed with blood in the left ventricle to carry the vital spirit around the body.

1643 Evangelista Torricelli (Italian) proved that air had weight and took up space.

late 1600s Robert Hooke, Robert Boyle, and John Mayow (English) showed that the substance in air that animals need is the same substance that makes a fire burn.

1771 Carl Scheele (Swedish) discovered oxygen.

late 1700s Antoine Lavoisier (French) and Joseph Priestley (English) demonstrated that oxygen is the vital component in air and is involved in producing energy in the body.

1837 Royal Humane Society in London recommended artificial respiration by pressure on chest wall; first enclosed diving suit was produced.

1846 First surgical operation under ether anesthesia (in Massachusetts General Hospital).

late 1800s Eduard Pflueger (German) showed that energy-producing reactions occur in body tissues; Claude Bernard (French) found that oxygen is delivered to body cells by red blood cells; John Haldane (English) studied breathing and developed methods to determine oxygen and carbon dioxide in blood and lungs.

early 1900s Otto Warburg (German) studied energy production in the tissues; Joseph Barcroft (English) found out how oxygen passes from the lungs into the blood.

1943 Jacques Cousteau (French) developed scuba-diving equipment.

1954 John Gibbon (American) used a heart-lung machine to take the place of the heart and lungs during surgery.

late 1950s Artificial respiration by blowing into the lungs became standard.

1964 The U.S. Surgeon General reported that smoking is dangerous to health.

1988 The U.S. Surgeon General reported that smoking is addictive.

1989 Artificial surfactant treatments of the lungs of premature babies became available and led to a sharp drop in death and health problems due to respiratory distress syndrome.

1989 Scientists found the gene involved in cystic fibrosis.

1994 Researchers inserted normal cystic fibrosis genes into human lung cells.

INDEX